More Jesus Diet
More of God, Less of Me, *Literally*

Robin Merrill

Welcome back!

In 2013, I published a collection of 30 devotions titled *The Jesus Diet: How the Holy Spirit Coached Me to a 50-Pound Weight Loss*. In this book, I shared about my own journey toward improved spiritual—and as a result, physical—health.

Now it is two years later. If I could have foreseen then what these two years would bring me, I might have crouched behind the couch with a bag of chocolate chips and just waited for the storm to pass. I guess that's why God didn't give me the gift of foresight.

You see, I've had a few difficult seasons since we've last talked. Some of these storms I have handled beautifully (if I do say so myself), completely leaning on my God and walking triumphantly as I did so. But other times, I wasn't so wise. Other times, I gave way to fear, anxiety, and grief. And there were times when I fell back into old eating habits as a way of comforting or medicating myself.

So, if you're looking to find me now, two years post-first book, as a size two bikini model, ha! That's not happening. There were days I had to run as fast as I could just to stay in one place. But if you're looking to find me now as someone still fighting the fight, still sure God will deliver me, one day at a time, then you've found her. I have had some hard days, but I thank God for them. I have never been so sure of my God's faithfulness as I am now. When I have sought him, I have found him, always with open arms.

The response to *The Jesus Diet* has been miraculous. I have met so many beloved brothers and sisters, and I thank God for each of you. I have been praying for your health, and if the Spirit prompts you to pray the same for me, I would be grateful.

To those new to *The Jesus Diet*, welcome. God wants you to be healthy. And he can make you healthy. All you have to do is let him. All you have to do is get yourself out of the way. As I continue to fight the fight, I invite you to join me. But remember, this is not about *me* telling *you* what to do. I simply want to share my testimony. Because if I can lose weight, *anyone can*—with God's help.

Big, big love,

~ Robin

Remember: This Is War

> For though we walk in the flesh, we do not war
> according to the flesh, for the weapons of our warfare
> are not of the flesh, but divinely powerful for the
> destruction of fortresses. (2 Corinthians 10:3–4)

Weight loss success began for me when I recognized my overeating as a spiritual battle. People have questioned this assertion. I have even second-guessed myself. An annoying little voice pops up and says something like, "Be reasonable Robin. There are no spiritual forces at work here. It's just an Oreo. You've really gone off the deep end."

But I think the Word is pretty clear. Our struggle is against the forces of darkness and the spiritual forces of wickedness (Eph. 6:12). Why wouldn't Satan want me miserable? Why wouldn't he want me tired and unhealthy? If he can keep us out of the fight with a few Twinkies, well then, he's got it made!

And if we recognize that this is indeed a spiritual battle, we also must recognize that we need to fight back spiritually. Paul writes that our weapons are not of the flesh. We must fight with weapons that have divine power. *Divine power!* How can we lose if we're fighting with divine power?

Lies take root in our hearts and flourish. They weave together to create seemingly impenetrable fortresses. We can't do something we want to do because of this stronghold of deception in our lives. We cannot destroy these spiritual fortresses with our own power. We need divine power.

We cannot fight spiritual battles with fleshly weapons (e.g., the latest fad diet or "miracle" pill). We must draw on the power of God, the power of the cross, the power of the Word to tear down these strongholds one by one. This is war, and when we pretend that it isn't, we lose.

Prayer:

Heavenly Father, I do not understand all that goes on in the spiritual realm, but I know that I don't have to. All I have to do is rely on you and your power. Please help me to do this, Father. Please arm me with your weaponry and help me to tear down the strongholds standing between us. Amen.

But, What Do You Eat?!

> There is nothing better for a man *than* to eat and drink
> and tell himself that his labor is good. This also I have
> seen that it is from the hand of God. (Ecclesiastes 2:24)

I've heard the question so many times, now it makes me laugh.
Since the publication of *The Jesus Diet*, people keep asking
me: *But what do you eat?!*

I apologize. I didn't mean to make this such a big mystery. It's
just that, I didn't really think it mattered *what* I ate. I stand by
my original statement that it's not so much about *what* I eat as
it is about the *state of my heart* while I'm eating. Am I
grateful? Am I putting God first? Am I at peace?

Part of having a spiritual approach to weight loss is *not* having
a legalistic one—a bunch of strict rules that will only make me
frustrated and bitter.

So my answer to this type of question often annoys the asker. I
say, "Anything." And that's almost true. Because I try to
involve God in every decision, in every bite, I usually end up
eating only when I'm truly hungry. And I usually try to avoid
junk food, as I know what a slippery slope that can be for me
(don't give the devil a foothold!). But these aren't rules.

The only "rule" of The Jesus Diet is this: Seek God first.

If you do that, you will be healthier. I promise.

Prayer:

Father, I've asked it before, but I need to ask it again. Please help me to put you first in every single decision I make. Whether it's what job I take, what words I say, what shows I watch, or what foods I eat. Thank you, Father, for caring about the details of my life. I love you. Amen.

Stop Underestimating the Power of God

> 'Ah Lord GOD! Behold, You have made the heavens and the earth by Your great power and by Your outstretched arm! Nothing is too difficult for You.' (Jeremiah 32:17)

I used to seriously underestimate God's power. I believed that God was real. I believed that he had raised his Son from the grave. I believed that he performed miracles thousands of years ago. But that's about where I stopped giving him credit. If someone testified about a miracle they had personally witnessed, I would roll my eyes and/or try to explain it away with science or reason.

I admit it. I was kind of a jerk. But stay with me. I get better.

Everything changed when I began to work for World Outreach International. I am an editor for WOI, which means that my inbox regularly fills up with dozens of testimonies from missionaries in the field, and it is my job to edit these testimonies into stories and articles for publication.

I remember that first month, sitting at my tiny crooked desk, sifting through these testimonies, thinking, *surely, all of these people can't be lying, I mean, they are* missionaries *after all. Missionaries don't lie, right? Right?!*

They weren't lying. To this day, my inbox continues to fill with miraculous accounts. People with terminal illnesses—healed. Alcoholics—sobered. Persecution—interrupted by a freak storm. Witch doctors—turned evangelists. Over and over, I read about God using his supernatural power. Today. Not yesterday. Not 2,000 years ago. Today. Right now.

We serve a God who created the heavens and the earth. We serve a God who raises people from the grave. Why would he suddenly stop being powerful? Why would he suddenly stop using his power?

I was putting God in a box. I was limiting him. And if I didn't believe in his power, I surely couldn't call on that power to change my life. If you too have put God in a box, I encourage you to let him out. Set him free and acknowledge the power that truly exists—the holy, supernatural power that can truly change you.

Prayer:

Sovereign God, I know in my heart that you are the God Almighty. I know that there is nothing too great for you. I know that with you, nothing is impossible. Please, Father, increase my faith in your power. And use that power to change me from the inside out. Amen.

Be You

> I will give thanks to You, for I am fearfully and
> wonderfully made;
> Wonderful are Your works,
> And my soul knows it very well. (Psalm 139:14)

Often, God has to tell me something over and over again before I get it. This is one of those times. About a year ago, my friend Zanne started saying to me, "Just be you."

This seems like such simple advice, but it was too complicated for me—at first.

I am sad to say that this writing world of mine can be competitive. And I was making decisions based on what other people would like to read, what others would like to hear; so Zanne said, "Stop it. Just be you."

Of course, I dismissed her advice, thinking that she was just being kind, thinking that being me couldn't possibly help me to accomplish what I wanted to accomplish. I needed to be more than me. I needed to be like other, more successful writers and poets. If I could be like *them*, then I would win. Then I would sell books. Then I would be a success.

Not long after, I was at SoulFest, sitting in the hot sun at Paul Colman's songwriters' workshop (which might be my favorite place to be in the whole wide world). I watched and listened as Paul mentored a young songwriter and musician. Paul said, and I paraphrase, "Don't do that. God made you *you*. So just be you."

It sounded so much like what Zanne had been saying to me that my ears perked up. You know what they say about coincidences? They take a lot of planning. So I went to the Word, and of course, you know what I found. *I* am fearfully and wonderfully made. And God doesn't make mistakes. God made me to be *me*, the way he designed me.

And as I meditated on this verse, I started to giggle, because something funny occurred to me. God made me to be *me*, nothing less, and nothing *more*.

I am fearfully and wonderfully made, but I've been hiding myself under layers of self-abuse. By overeating, I've been messing with God's design.

I don't want to do that anymore. It's so cool that I am fearfully and wonderfully made. I'm going to start acting like I'm aware of (and grateful for) that fact.

Prayer:

Almighty Creator, thank you for designing me. Thank you for making me *me*. Forgive me when I don't act like the *me* you made me to be. Help me to be the person you made me to be, nothing less, and nothing more. Amen.

Devote Yourself to Prayer

> Devote yourselves to prayer, keeping alert in it with *an attitude of* thanksgiving (Colossians 4:2)

I think we all know we're supposed to pray. That's no secret. Yet how many of us are confident that our prayer lives are as healthy as they can be? As they should be?

Paul tells us to *devote* ourselves to prayer. Devote is a pretty strong word. You can't "devote" something halfway (or a third of the way). Devote means all in.

Sometimes I don't do a very good job of devoting myself to prayer. In fact, when I find myself getting off track with my eating, if I'm honest and ask myself, "Self, how is your prayer life?" Well, then my self can always say, "Not good."

I've found a direct correspondence between my prayer life and my physical health. If you're looking for a boost to your battle plan, I encourage you to devote yourself to prayer.

It's not as if your efforts will be wasted. Jesus Christ himself said, "If you ask Me anything in My name, I will do it." He will do it. He will help you win your battle. He will do it because he loves you and because he wants to glorify his Father.

(And if you haven't seen *War Room*, see it right now, and skip the popcorn.)

Prayer:

Jesus, please let your Holy Spirit urge me to pray throughout the day. I want to devote myself to prayer. Help me to do so. Take away any distractions and help me to remain connected with you at all times. Amen.

A Living Sacrifice

> Therefore I urge you, brethren, by the mercies of God, to present your bodies a living and holy sacrifice, acceptable to God, which is your spiritual service of worship. (Romans 12:1)

My spiritual service. The King James calls it "reasonable service." My understanding here is that, in light of all God has done for me (the mercies), the only reasonable thing for me to do is to spiritually offer myself, my body, as a living and holy sacrifice.

I don't do this every day. I should. I'm trying. But I often fail.

How different might my life be if I lived every single second as though I were sacrificing it to God? How would it feel to live with complete selflessness? I'll probably never get there in this lifetime. But I want to try.

Worship is not just throwing my arms up in the air and singing along to a peppy tune. Worship is a *service*. It's about me giving back to God.

Now, if I want to offer my *body* as a spiritual sacrifice, then I want to offer Jesus the best body I can, a body that is able to be his hands and feet, a body that glorifies him, a healthy, able body. So I had better get to work.

Prayer:

Father, thank you for your mercies. I do want to offer my body to you, every day, every second, as a living sacrifice. Help me to do just that, and help me to have a body worth offering. Amen.

Excuses

> The sluggard says, "There is a lion outside; I will be killed in the streets!" (Proverbs 22:13)

I'll admit: this verse stumped me at first. I couldn't figure out why a sluggard would say this. Then, when I finally got it, I laughed out loud. The sluggard doesn't want to go outside, so he says he will be killed by a lion. What a *lame* excuse! Ha!

I am the *queen* of excuses. I am a prolific excuse-generator: *I was sad. I had a hard day. It's raining out. Someone criticized the worship music.* You get the drift.

Sure, I'm not claiming there's a lion out to eat me, but still, my excuses are pretty lame. And I don't think God wants me trying to make excuses. I don't think he wants me rationalizing my bad decisions.

As long as I'm justifying my poor choices, I am not working to correct them.

So, if you're not the excuse-making type, good for you! But if you're like me, I challenge you to try to catch yourself making up lions at your door.

There were no lions in the sluggard's street. Sadness does not merit a whoopie pie. A hard day can be improved with a salad. In truth, it stopped raining at noon. The worship music was pretty bad. You get the drift.

Prayer:

Jesus, thank you for your patience with me. Please help me to catch myself when I'm rationalizing irrational ideas, whether I'm doing it to myself, to others, or to you. Please help me to be honest and transparent every day. Amen.

I'll Start (Again) Tomorrow

> Behold, now is "THE ACCEPTABLE TIME," behold,
> now is "THE DAY OF SALVATION"
> (2 Corinthians 6:2b)

These words are in all caps because Paul was quoting from Isaiah (49:8), not because he was screaming at us. Though maybe screaming would be effective for some of us: THE TIME IS NOW! WAKE UP!

My understanding of Paul here is that there is no better time to accept God's grace than *right this second*.

Have you ever said, "I'll start tomorrow" or "I'll get back on track tomorrow" or "I'll start on January 1"?

Every single time I've said this, I've lied. It just doesn't work for me to "start tomorrow." I'm only ever able to grow spiritually when I start the second the thought occurs to me, even if that thought occurs to me halfway through my third Twizzler.

In fact, I'm pretty sure that I've planned to start tomorrow at least a hundred tomorrows in a row.

I've come to realize that promising myself that I'll "get back on track tomorrow" is just a way of rationalizing today's selfishness.

So if you're guilty of this too, I invite you to join me in starting *today*. Right now.

Prayer:

Father, forgive me for procrastination. I want to get back on track with you right this second. I want to live within your will right now. Please give my heart a sense of urgency. Amen.

Work It

> Then the LORD God took the man and put him into the garden of Eden to cultivate it and keep it. (Genesis 2:15)

To cultivate it. The ESV and NIV write: "to work it." The NKJV translates: "to tend it." The point is: the Garden of Eden did not take care of itself.

Even before the fall, humans were designed for physical labor. It was not a punishment. It was a gift. Adam and Eve were placed in paradise and were given a job to do: a *physical* job.

Today, many of us work for a living without using our bodies much at all. My fingers get a terrific workout at the keyboard, but if I don't make an effort outside of my profession, a daily eight hours of finger aerobics is about the only exercise my body would get. And that's just not going to cut it.

In *The Jesus Diet* and in my own battle with overeating, I focus on the consumption of calories a lot more than I do the burning of them, because that's where I most struggle, but both sides of the equation matter.

God didn't design us to sit (or lie) around as if we're trying to keep our furniture from running off. He gave us bodies that *need* to exercise. That's why we're so much happier and healthier when we do.

So find a way: walk, jog, run, dance, tend your own garden— just keep moving.

Prayer:

Father, thank you for designing me with the ability to exercise. Please motivate me to stay moving. Amen.

The Opposition

> At whatever place you hear the sound of the trumpet,
> rally to us there. Our God will fight for us.
> (Nehemiah 4:20)

Nehemiah and his fellow Jews decided to rebuild the wall around Jerusalem. This was no small task, and the only way to do it was one block at a time.

But these folks had more than the hard work to contend with. Of course, they had naysayers. They had critics. They had bullies.

We see it here and we see it throughout history. You've likely seen it in your own life: any work for God will face opposition.

Some dude said to Nehemiah, "Your wall is so weak, a fox could knock it over" (v. 3). You may know someone with an equally dazzling sense of humor.

As I work toward better health, I am rebuilding something. And I am doing it one stone at a time. And there are naysayers. There are critics. There are even bullies.

This only confirms what I already know: God wants me to be healthy, so of course there will be opposition. But that doesn't mean I have to give in to it. Nehemiah didn't. Those Jews stood strong and the wall got built.

We can model our own behavior after theirs. We can expect opposition, and deal with it wisely when we face it. Because, just as God did for the Jews, he will fight for us.

Prayer:

Father, I don't even know why I fear people and what they have to say. Help me to be brave in the face of ridicule. Help me to only hear your voice. Thank you for fighting for me. Amen.

The Desires of Your Heart

> Trust in the LORD and do good;
> Dwell in the land and cultivate faithfulness.
> Delight yourself in the LORD ;
> And He will give you the desires of your heart.
> (Psalm 37:3-4)

Cultivate faithfulness. Live in the land and work the ground in order to raise crops—good, healthy, abundant crops of faithfulness. The New King James translates this verse to "feed on His faithfulness." His faithfulness sustains us. And when we *feed* our lives, feed our hearts on faithfulness, when we *delight* in the Lord, he will give us what our hearts desire.

Delight yourself—what do you delight yourself in? If we seek God, we will find him so wholly that we can't help but delight in him! Imagine the delight of walking hand in hand with the Creator of the universe. We can do that in our daily lives! I so often forget that, and don't strive for it, don't seek him enough, but it is when I do seek him that he will give me the desires of my heart.

So what does my heart truly desire? It truly desires the peace of God, and the health and safety of my family. My heart wants to love and be loved. My heart desires to be useful to the Kingdom. My heart wants to honor and glorify my Creator.

My heart does *not* want a third helping of macaroni and cheese. It's not my true heart that wants the pizza buffet or the entire pint of Ben & Jerry's. So why am I seeking these things?

Prayer:

Father, thank you for your faithfulness. Thank you for being willing to grant me the desires of my heart. Please help me to be aware of what my heart truly desires. Thank you, Father. I want to walk hand in hand with you today and every day. Amen.

New Mercies

The steadfast love of the LORD never ceases;
his mercies never come to an end;
they are new every morning;
great is your faithfulness. (Lamentations 3:22-23)

Here it is: I have to work late. To keep myself awake, I absentmindedly munch on crackers at my desk (for about five hours). Finally! I meet the deadline. It is time for bed, but I'm so wound up with adrenalin that I need to unwind. And I should celebrate, right? Someone left some cake at my house after Bible study. I should go polish that off, right?

In the morning, I can scarcely drag myself out of bed because I feel so saturated with shame.

Well, how silly is that? I shouldn't have wasted energy on guilt. I should have opened my eyes and burst into praise for the morning! Because every morning gifts us with brand spankin' new mercies!

Every morning, God's mercies offer us a clean slate. We get to start over. What we did yesterday has been washed away by the blood of Jesus. We can leap out of bed and declare victory over the day ahead.

So if you do slip up, or even if you trip and fall down the mountain as I've done a few times, don't fear. The sun will come up in the morning, and with it God's mercies will shine down on you!

Prayer:

Father, thank you for your mercies. Thank you that even when I make bad decisions, the war is still won. Help me to embrace each morning as a new chance to glorify you! Amen.

Humility vs. Self-Esteem

> He has told you, O man, what is good;
> And what does the LORD require of you
> But to do justice, to love kindness,
> And to walk humbly with your God? (Micah 6:8)

I love it when God makes things simple. What does God want from us? To do justice, love kindness, and walk humbly with him. But the walking humbly part is easier said than done.

I once heard a pastor say, "If anyone says they are good at humility, they're lying."

For a long time I thought I was "good at humility" because I pretty much hated myself. But low self-esteem and humility are not the same thing.

Low self-esteem is a trick of the enemy. Low self-esteem is believing that you are unlovable. Humility is recognizing who you are in Jesus, who you are in front of Jesus, and *admitting how much you need his love.*

To be truly humble, we need to *let Jesus love us.* True humility is being willing to accept his love no matter how much it will change you.

Prayer:

God, help me to walk humbly with you. Help me to know who I am in you, who you created me to be. I know you don't make mistakes. Please pour your love into me and help me to accept it all. Amen.

Control Freak

> And we know that God causes all things to work
> together for good to those who love God, to those who
> are called according to His purpose. (Romans 8:28)

I used to be a real control freak. (OK, to be completely honest,
sometimes I still am.)

At some point in my life, I decided that I was in charge of my
own life and that it was up to me to make sure everything went
smoothly. I didn't consult God. Instead, I assumed that I knew
what I wanted, and that it was up to me to make sure I got
what I wanted. This often involved trying to control other
people. This often involved trying to manipulate
circumstances. This was a difficult and exhausting way to live.

"God is in control" was a completely foreign concept to me,
even though I had spent much of my life as a believer. I did not
know that I could rest in God's arms. I didn't know that I could
"let go and let God" take charge of my life.

I remember specific instances of me freaking out because
things were spiraling so completely *out of* control. Marriage
was hard. Pregnancy was hard. Injury had me immobile in the
hospital. My boss was being mean. I kept finding myself in
situations I just couldn't *fix*. This frustrated me, the control
freak, to no end. And to make myself feel better, to restore
some semblance of control to the situation, I would eat.

I may not have been able to control my situation, but I sure
could control what I put in my mouth. And I thought that's
what I was doing. I would eat spitefully, knowing it was going
against doctor's orders. I would overeat as if I was "showing
them" who was in charge (whoever "them" may be).

Obviously, I was not in control. I didn't see it then, *but food
was in control of me.*

When I stopped trying to control my life, my life improved miraculously. When I stopped trying to get people to behave the way I wanted, *I* began to behave the way I wanted. I was blown away that something as simple as *surrender* could change things so drastically.

Prayer:

Father, I know you are in control. Please help me to surrender every aspect of my life so that you may do with me as you wish. I know that your plans are better than my plans. Thy will be done. Amen.

Fear Is a Thief

> For God has not given us a spirit of timidity, but of power and love and discipline. (2 Timothy 1:7)

The Greek word here translated "timidity" is *deilia*, which *Strong's* defines as "timidity, fearfulness, cowardice." Not a pretty picture. This is not the fear of God that brings wisdom. This is me cowering behind the couch, afraid of the boogieman.

Can I ask you an odd question? Are you afraid of being healthy? Are you afraid of being thin? I talk to people about weight loss a lot these days and I keep hearing this fear theme repeated. People are afraid of losing weight.

If you aren't afraid of being healthier, that's great news! Feel free to skip to the next page. If you *are* afraid, then I invite you to ask yourself *why*? What are you afraid of? Are you afraid of failing? Are you afraid you won't be able to keep the weight off?

I have come to realize that, at times, I have been afraid that I would go to all this work to lose all this weight and that I still wouldn't like myself. Pretty scary stuff.

I don't know what you are afraid of, or if you are even afraid of anything. What I do know is that God's love is the opposite of fear. Love and fear cannot operate at the same time. One will always beat out the other. But we get to decide which wins.

God says, do not be afraid! He has you! If you are living in fear of something, recognize that this something is far inferior to an almighty God.

Give your fears to God and make room in your heart for his perfect love. Perfect love casts out fear (1 John 4:18).

Prayer:

Almighty God, my fears must seem so silly to you. Please make them seem silly to me too. Please crush my fears with your love. Please make me brave. Amen.

Sleep Is a Gift

> It is vain for you to rise up early,
> To retire late,
> To eat the bread of painful labors;
> For He gives to His beloved even in his sleep.
> (Psalm 127:2)

Joan works two jobs. She gets up before the sunrise and stays up past midnight. Some days, she functions on only one or two hours of sleep. She is miserable. She is unhealthy. And she's not even getting anywhere. All her toil seems to be in vain.

It is.

I'm not saying that we shouldn't work hard. God wants us to work hard and do our best (Col. 3:23). But some of us are working ourselves to death, and I don't think that's the way God planned it.

We *need* sleep. He designed us this way. Sleep is healthy. People who get enough sleep are drastically healthier and happier than those who don't. They feel better physically, mentally, and emotionally. They are better equipped to serve God and to serve others.

When I don't get enough sleep, I am primed to overeat. I eat for energy, energy that I am lacking because of my lack of sleep. When I make a healthy amount of sleep a priority, I eat healthier by default.

Matthew Henry wrote that sleep is "God's gift to his beloved." I agree.

Prayer:

Dear God, please help me to get a healthy amount of sleep.
Please help me to fall asleep when I am tired and to wake up
rested. Thank you for the gift of sleep. Amen.

Find Someone to Disciple

> The things which you have heard from me in the
> presence of many witnesses, entrust these to faithful
> men who will be able to teach others also.
> (2 Timothy 2:2)

God's family tree is supposed to look more like a spider web
than a spider. We should be discipling one another as much as
possible, in every direction, not relying on one pastor (the
body of the spider) to teach the few that he or she can reach
(the eight legs).

I spent years believing the lie that I wasn't a "good enough
Christian" to disciple others. What a bunch of horsefeathers!
I've come to understand that it's not about being "good
enough." None of us are good enough—that's why we need
Christ.

It's this simple: I have experienced the love of God, and that
means I have something to share.

Not long ago, I asked God to point me toward someone I could
disciple. And he did. Two beautiful, amazing young women
came into my life and we have formed fantastic relationships,
but God did something else that I wasn't expecting. He put me
in a position to disciple some people who had been discipling
me. This is what I mean by spider web. Discipling isn't
necessarily a top-down model. We should be ready to disciple
anyone who needs it, at any time.

When I began consciously discipling others, something pretty amazing happened. I became a whole lot more accountable. It scared me at first, but it's more sobering than scary. *People were watching me.* They were watching to see if my actions matched my words. Sometimes they do. Sometimes they don't, but I sure work harder at being consistent when I know people are paying attention.

Discipling others will spread the Kingdom of God. Doing so is obviously good for the Kingdom. But it'll also be good for *you.*

Prayer:

Father in Heaven, please remove any inhibitions I have about discipling others. Please show me people I can help grow in you. I want to help your Kingdom grow! Amen.

Ask Someone to Pray for You

> Therefore, confess your sins to one another, and pray for one another so that you may be healed. The effective prayer of a righteous man can accomplish much. (James 5:16)

Speaking of accountability, have you asked anyone to pray for you yet? I read this verse and I hear God say, "Tell someone in what area you're struggling, and ask for prayer."

I'll be completely honest: the first time I asked for prayer in regards to overeating, it didn't go so well. I called up a great friend who is an amazing woman of God and I said, "I need your help. I am really focusing on my eating right now. I am abusing food and I need to get this under control. Could you please pray for me?"

And she said something along the lines of "Ha! You and me both sister!"

It was hard for her to take such a request seriously. She didn't know that this issue had me face down on the floor. In her experience, this just wasn't an issue that required fervent prayer.

I don't share this part of my story to shame my friend. She is an awesome friend. I tell you so that if you get a similar response, you will know that you simply need to ask someone else. Because the second person I asked, well that conversation went much differently.

To the second friend I said, "I'm really struggling with anxiety and eating right now and I could use some prayer."

And she said, "I'm going to my knees for you right now."

This response stole my breath away.

She was going to her knees? Like, literally?

If my friend was actually kneeling before the God of the universe in the middle of the daytime on my behalf, well then I guess I had better take my own request pretty seriously. And I was driven straight to the Word for more searching and more strength.

After about an hour, I texted her a quick, "thank you" to which she replied, "still praying." *That's* the kind of prayer support you need! Not only will God hear these prayers from your brothers and sisters, but these prayers will help you be honest with yourself. When I know someone is praying for me, I pay extra close attention to my own heart. I can't help but do so.

Prayer:

Thank you, Father for the gift of prayer. Please show me prayer warriors whom I can ask for prayer support. Please also encourage others to ask me for prayer support, so that I can go to my knees for another one of your children. Amen.

One (Tenth of a) Pound at a Time

> The Lord your God will clear away these nations before you little by little; you will not be able to put an end to them quickly, for the wild beasts would grow too numerous for you. (Deuteronomy 7:22)

I get frustrated when the scale does not greet my morning grimace with miraculous numbers. I have worked hard, and I want to see dramatic results! But as we know, it usually doesn't work that way.

God promised to drive out Israel's enemies from the land little by little. Otherwise, all the Canaanites would leave, and the land would be overrun with wildlife. Notice the use of the word "beasts" though. Not the cute, innocent wildlife. The wild beasts.

If losing weight were a quick process, would you really be prepared for the results? I know I wouldn't be. If I didn't have to work at weight loss, little by little, one (tenth of a) pound at a time, I would be ill-equipped to deal with beasts like pride, low self-esteem, lack of trust, and impatience.

God is shaping us into the people he wants us to be. He chooses to do this little by little for a reason. His timing is perfect. I shouldn't be upset when the scales don't shout big numbers at me. I should be focused on the fact that I am a work in progress. And as long as I'm progressing in the right direction, then that is miracle enough.

Prayer:

Father, thank you for helping me through this weight loss process. Thank you for shaping me little by little. Help me to be patient. Help me to have faith in your plan, and your timing. Amen.

Trichotomy

> Then God said, "Let Us make man in Our image,
> according to Our likeness" (Genesis 1:26a)

If we start reading the Bible from the beginning, this is the
first we hear of the Trinity: God, Jesus, and the Holy Spirit.

We are created like the Trinity in that we are trichotomous
beings. I have spent most of my life as a believer without this
knowledge. I'm not sure how I missed it, but for the longest
time, I did not understand that there were three parts of me:
body, soul, spirit.

Here's how I've come to understand it:

The body is the easy part for us to be aware of. That's the part
with big pores, stretch marks, and aches and pains.

The soul is the "personality" part of me. It's my will. It's my
thoughts. My soul is the part of me that makes me "me," that
makes me different from you. No two souls are alike.

The spirit is the part of me that sprang to life the second the
Holy Spirit entered me. My spirit is the part of me that allows
me to have a personal relationship with the God of the
universe.

In my understanding, all three parts will go on to eternity,
though we will get new bodies. (I'm believing for a size 8.)

Why does all this matter? Once I realized that there were three
parts of me, I realized I had to surrender all three.

I couldn't just surrender my spirit. I also had to surrender my
will and my body.

I couldn't just surrender my body. That was impossible without also surrendering my will and my spirit.

We are all going through the sanctification process. This is a transformation. But if I don't surrender all three parts of myself to this process, my transformation will be significantly slowed down, if not halted altogether.

God made us this way: body, soul, spirit; he wants us to give *all* of ourselves back to him. If we truly want transformation, this is the only way.

Prayer:

Father, thank you for making me in the image of the Trinity. I surrender to you completely. I give you my physical body. I give you my soul—my will, my thoughts, my personality—to mold as you wish. I give you my spirit, that part of me that knows you intimately. Thank you, Father for making this existence so glorious! Amen.

Food as Idol

> For the LORD your God is a consuming fire, a jealous God. (Deuteronomy 4:24)

I can't speak for you, but I'm not thrilled with the idea of God as consuming fire. But, this is the truth, so I guess the best plan would be for me to not make him jealous.

I've never really felt convicted of idolatry. I don't make statues and bow down to them. I don't pray to pagan gods.

But I have chosen a meal out after church over putting money in the offering plate. I have chosen to silence the voice of the Holy Spirit when he urges me not to indulge. I have chosen to overeat while a brother or sister goes hungry.

The reality is that I have chosen food over God—over and over again.

The fact that God is a jealous God should be comforting. He loves me. He wants me all to himself. And when I don't let him have me, when I continue to choose my fleshly wants over his will, I might as well be bowing down before the golden calf.

And I don't want to do that. Because that seems silly. And if I'm really honest, worshipping food is pretty silly too.

Prayer:

Father, you are the only one, true God, and I know this. Help me to remember that you are jealous for me. Help me to take comfort in this knowledge. Help me to never put anything ahead of you. Amen.

Food as Master

> No servant can serve two masters; for either he will hate the one and love the other, or else he will be devoted to one and despise the other. You cannot serve God and wealth. (Luke 16:13)

This is Jesus talking. *Jesus*. You remember him? The King of the universe? And he's telling us it is *impossible* to serve two masters. Many of us know this verse. Most of us get it. It's not too complicated. You can't serve both God and money at the same time. But it has occurred to me that you can replace "wealth" with anything else.

You cannot serve both God and fear.

You cannot serve both God and addiction.

You cannot serve both God and food.

Food has been my undisputed master for many years. And it's been a cruel taskmaster. And I didn't realize that by serving food, by putting my fleshly wants first, I was directly *not* serving God. I guess, if I had thought about it at all, I figured I *could* do both. But by living like this, I was calling Jesus a liar. Because, we *can't* do both. He says so.

I don't want to serve money. I don't want to serve fear. I don't want to serve flour and sugar. I want to serve only God, the one who made me, the one who has put up with me all these years, the one who died on the cross for me. *That* Master. If I can only choose one, I want it to be him.

Prayer:

Father, please show me in my daily life those moments when I am trying to serve someone or something other than you. Help me to always put you first, every second of every day. Amen.

I Do the Very Thing I Do Not Want to Do

> For what I am doing, I do not understand; for I am not practicing what I *would* like to *do*, but I am doing the very thing that I hate. (Romans 7:15-20)

When I read these verses, I think the Apostle Paul must be hiding somewhere in my living room watching me eat chocolate chips straight out of the bag.

I can't speak for you, but sometimes I look at myself and think, "Why am I doing this? This is not what I want to do!" and yet I keep doing it.

Obviously, Paul knew what it was to struggle with the flesh. And I find tremendous comfort in this. Paul willingly admitted that he struggled to avoid temptation. That sometimes he did things that he didn't even want to do, that he knew were wrong, but he did them anyway: because *the flesh is weak*.

This doesn't excuse Paul, and it doesn't excuse us. But look at what God did with Paul. He brought the Gospel to the Gentiles. (That's me. That might well be you too.) He brought the Gospel to the corners of his world. He wrote (at least) *thirteen* books of the Bible. Can you even imagine the New Testament without Paul? By the power of God, the testimony of a single man has influenced literally *millions* of people in the last two thousand years.

Paul was not perfect. Paul struggled, just like I do. But God used him mightily. I want God to use me too.

Prayer:

Father, thank you for the encouraging example of Paul. Please help my flesh to die and your Spirit to win. Please protect me from doing the very thing I do not want to do. Amen.

Little Eyes Are Watching

> The LORD is slow to anger and abundant in lovingkindness, forgiving iniquity and transgression; but He will by no means clear *the guilty*, visiting the iniquity of the fathers on the children to the third and fourth generations. (Numbers 14:18)

Bible readers disagree about exactly how generational curses do or do not play out in our world. But most agree on this one common sense principle: our actions have consequences that can affect our children.

My daughter is watching me right now. She is observing my attitude, my behavioral patterns, my priorities. That chills me to the bone. She may, willingly or unconsciously, imitate my behavior. She will likely pick up my habits. She may fall into my patterns.

And someday she will have children, who will watch her the way she has watched me. In this way, our iniquities can and do affect the generations to come. Scary stuff.

How can we teach our children not to be addicts? How can we train them not to overeat? Not with scales, calculators, and pushups. No. We do it with our own behavior. We do it with our own decisions.

Overeating has wreaked havoc on my life. I won't let it wreak havoc on my daughter's.

Prayer:

Father, motivate me to obey you. Help me to protect my children and my children's children from the consequences that come from not listening to your voice. Amen.

Look at the Birds

> Look at the birds of the air, that they do not sow, nor reap nor gather into barns, and *yet* your heavenly Father feeds them. Are you not worth much more than they? (Matthew 6:26)

The Jesus Diet has made me many new friends and I have heard countless stories from brothers and sisters all over the world. And I've noticed a recurring theme: some people are just trying to avoid hunger.

An amazing godly woman told me about her difficult childhood, how she had often not had enough to eat. Now, she regularly overeats. She wondered if there was a connection. I wondered, how could there not be?

Others shared with me how they get into trouble when they encounter "free food," be it a buffet, a church pot luck, or a gifted restaurant meal. It's as if they think, *I need to get my money's worth.*

Don't get me wrong. I can understand all of this. But if you are having similar experiences, I want to encourage you: God isn't going to let you starve. Consider the Israelites with their miraculous manna. God didn't let them stockpile. They had to get their manna every day so that they would learn to rely on God *every day*. We don't have to try to "get our money's worth." We can just trust God to give us what we need each and every day. I know, it's easier said than done, but we can do it. The more we trust God, the more he will prove to us he is worthy of it. And if it makes it any easier, you can always avoid potlucks.

Prayer:

Thank you, Father, for your provision. Help me to trust in you to meet my daily needs. Thank you for your trustworthiness. Amen.

Anger

> And Jesus entered the temple and drove out all those
> who were buying and selling in the temple, and
> overturned the tables of the money changers and the
> seats of those who were selling doves. And He said to
> them, "It is written, 'MY HOUSE SHALL BE CALLED A
> HOUSE OF PRAYER'; but you are making it a
> ROBBERS' DEN." (Matthew 21:12-13)

I am no stranger to anger. In the past, intense, chronic anger
has taken me to dark places.

And I've gotten into some (loving) debates with some of my
godly friends when I say that I don't think anger is inherently
wrong.

There is a lot to be angry about in this world, in this life. I
don't see how anger in itself can be an offense against God. I
do see, however, that how we handle anger might take us over
the line. I'm angry. OK, so what am I going to do about it?
How is that anger going to manifest itself?

Jesus had righteous anger. The people in the temple were
dishonoring his father. He was mad. But he did two things
with his anger: 1) he took practical action, and 2) he used
words.

This is not how I've processed anger for most of my life.
Instead, I have shoved anger deep down inside. I did this
because I thought "good Christian girls shouldn't get angry."
And I did this because I was so terrified of hurting someone
else's feelings that I kept all the fury to myself. I pushed it deep
into my heart and then I tried to kill it.

I tried to kill it with food. Something in this crazy unfair life would make me angry, and instead of taking practical action to change the circumstances, instead of using words to express myself, I would go hide in my closet and eat a bacon hoagie. This would calm me down. This would make me feel better. This would help me hide my anger.

Ha! How ridiculous is this?! If I'm not careful, I will still do this, but I'm trying desperately to follow Jesus' example. Step #1: Is there something I could do to change this circumstance? Step #2: Can I use the language God gave me to peacefully express myself?

It's also worth noting that Jesus didn't lose his cool and freak out on the money changers. Every action he took had *purpose*. He didn't fly off the handle—he was always in control of himself. It's a difficult example to follow, but will you join me in trying?

Prayer:

Father, I do get angry sometimes. Help me to know when this is righteous anger or simply selfish rubbish. When it is justified, please help to express my anger in a way that is healthy and safe for me and others, and glorifying to you. Amen.

Do Not Be Conformed

> And do not be conformed to this world, but be transformed by the renewing of your mind, so that you may prove what the will of God is, that which is good and acceptable and perfect. (Romans 12:2)

In the last year, I've had two very similar experiences. Each time, I was chatting with someone from another country. Each time, this person made a statement that startled me. One of them said, "Americans are a bunch of gluttons." The other one said, "This whole country is obese."

Don't get me wrong. I know that the Apostle Paul was not referring to American health when he penned his letter to the Romans. But I do believe that he was saying that those who follow Christ should stand out from those who don't.

After the second conversation of this nature, I had a mini-vision. What if all of Jesus' people sought to glorify him with their diets? What if all of us, across this country and in every other country, spiritualized our eating? What if Christians were "the healthy ones"?

Wouldn't we stand out then!

"Oh, well she's just skinny because she's a Christian." Ha!

I don't think "the will of God is" that Jesus' followers be roly-poly walking heart attacks (talking about myself here). I don't think "the will of God is" to have me too tired, too ashamed, too unhealthy to serve him and to serve others.

If we are following Paul's teaching and truly trying to "prove what the will of God is," then we must be putting God first in everything. Even our eating.

Prayer:

Father, I want to make you proud of me. I want to stand out for you. Please help me to not be conformed to this world. I want to glorify you and your good, acceptable, and perfect will. Amen.

I Found My Kitchen

> She rises also while it is still night
> And gives food to her household
> And portions to her maidens. (Proverbs 31:15)

Holy Scripture does not depict the excellent wife as punching the snooze button and then microwaving instant cereal. Go figure.

Granted, she didn't have access to microwaves, but even if she did, I don't think Proverbs would have gone there. But I'm not out to bash microwaves. Or snooze buttons.

My point is that here in Proverbs, getting up early to prepare food for the family was a lauded act. And I think this principle can apply to anyone, not just the wife/mother figure.

When it comes to the kitchen, I'm a bit of an anomaly. My mother was a professional. She worked full-time, and then spent every spare second of her time driving all over the state to deliver us kids to various sporting events. She was a home economics major, so I know she had the kitchen chops, but my memories indicate she didn't have much time to use them. While I do remember the elaborate Christmas shrimp gumbo, I also remember many, many cans of ravioli. And I'm not complaining. She didn't have *time* to cook.

Then I went to college, where I dined in a cafeteria. Then, I went straight from college to the merchant marine. For five years, I lived on ships (much like the merchant ships in the previous verse) and various men were paid to cook for me.

So, when I finally got married and walked into my first kitchen, I didn't know how to boil an egg. And then I too became a professional. I worked at least 40 hours a week. I didn't have time to cook. I didn't have the knowledge or skills. And I certainly didn't have the energy.

When I began focusing on my health though, I discovered something pretty drastic: cooking for myself makes it easier to eat healthy. I know, right?! Big news! Now, I'm still not a very good cook. But I do know how to boil an egg. And I've discovered that spending time in the kitchen is good for me spiritually.

And what I'm trying to share here has nothing to do with sexism. My wonderful husband cooks too. My point is that I think God wanted me to slow down, to learn how to take care of myself and my family. I think God wanted me to be able to boil my own eggs.

Prayer:

Father, I thank you and praise you that I am able to prepare food for myself and my family. Help me to do this for your glory. Help me to find the time and the energy to create healthy meals and snacks. Amen.

Contentment

> My soul is satisfied as with marrow and fatness,
> And my mouth offers praises with joyful lips.
> (Psalm 63:5)

At the beginning of this song, King David writes, "You are my God; I shall seek You earnestly."

When King David sought God, his soul was satisfied.

I never really considered myself a discontented person. I always knew keeping up with the Joneses was a lost cause. But the more time I spend in the Word, the more I realize I'm nowhere near as content as I could be, as I should be.

In my life, especially in the last few years, it seems I'm always in the middle of some crisis, either my own or someone else's. It seems I'm always begging God to "fix this," "save this," "heal this," or "stop this." I don't look around at the painful circus I'm in and think, "Wow, I am so content."

Yet, that's exactly what I should do. I should always be content because my personal Savior is in charge of every situation. He knows what's best and he can, and will, interfere when he needs to.

I think that I overeat sometimes to force a sense of artificial contentment, of physical fullness. Some people pursue power, affluence, status, possessions, or wealth to achieve contentment. I pursue chocolate chip cookies. But I'm not supposed to. I'm supposed to seek God, and find my fullness there.

The Apostle Paul wrote of being content in *all* circumstances. And that dude was chained, stoned, and shipwrecked! Yet he wrote "I have learned the secret of being filled and going hungry" (Phil. 4:12). This secret is contentment in Christ.

So next time I feel discontented, I'm going to reach for the Word, not the fridge.

Prayer:

Father, I'm so used to being discontented, I don't even really know what contentment feels like. Please show me. I am seeking you right now, and I ask you to show yourself to me. Amen.

For a Little While

> In this you greatly rejoice, even though now for a little while, if necessary, you have been distressed by various trials (1 Peter 1:6)

It's easy to read this verse and skip over the two little words: if necessary. I can't help but wonder if my trials are necessary. Even the ones I've directly caused myself. Maybe these trials are forming me into the woman God wants me to be, the woman he can use for something. Peter doesn't use the words "if by chance" or "if God was in the right mood." He uses the words "if necessary." It is necessary for me to learn these lessons, to endure these difficult seasons.

If there is nothing else to find comfort in, it is this: these difficult seasons are almost over.

And my battle with overeating is not an eternal one. I'm fairly confident neither you nor I will be counting calories in heaven.

Instead, we are going to be rocking new "heavenly bodies," bodies that will not get sick or injured (1 Cor. 15:53), bodies that will not suffer the effects of grief and pain (Rev. 21:4). Jesus is going to "transform the body of our humble state into conformity with the body of His glory" (Phil. 3:21). We will be strong (1 Cor. 15:53), raised in power and glory (1 Cor. 15:43).

This suffering that we are currently enduring, whatever it is: physical limitations, mental illness, family conflict, grief, sickness, addiction—*whatever* it is, it will be *gone*. Peter, bless his soul, uses the words "for a little while." That means, in the big picture, we are truly almost done with this battle. The end is near. We just need to hold on!

Prayer:

Father, help me to see the big picture. Help me to trust in your will and your timing. Thank you, Almighty Father, for the promise of heaven. Thank you for reserving me a spot in your paradise. Amen.

More Jesus Diet Soundtrack

"Day 1" by Matthew West

"The Best Is Yet to Come" by Paul Colman

"Whom Shall I Fear (God of Angel Armies)" by Chris Tomlin

"Dead Man (Carry Me)" by Jars of Clay

"Everything Glorious" by Dave Crowder Band

"How He Loves" by Dave Crowder Band

"No Thief Like Fear" by Jason Gray

"Overcomer" by Mandisa

"Shackles" by Mandisa

"Stronger" by Mandisa

"Good Morning" by Mandisa

"Thrive" by Casting Crowns

"Same Power" by Jeremy Camp

"Flawless" by MercyMe

"Move" by MercyMe

Made in the USA
Lexington, KY
17 May 2019